4th GRADE READING COMPREHENSION WORKBOOK

Daily Short Stories and Passages to Boost Fluency, Vocabulary & Critical Thinking for Ages 9-10 (in Print and Ebook Formats)

DR. FANATOMY
★★★★★

NAME : ....

copyright@ dr. fanatomy 2025

All rights reserved. No part of this publication may be reproduced, distributed, or transmitted in any form or by any means, including photocopying, recording, or other electronic or mechanical methods, without the prior written permission of the publisher, except in the case of brief quotations embodied in critical reviews and certain other noncommercial uses permitted by copyright law.

This book is a work of non-fiction, and any resemblance to actual persons, living or dead, or actual events is purely coincidental.

The information and techniques described in this book are intended for educational and informational purposes only. The author and publisher shall not be held liable for any injury, damage, or loss arising from using or misusing the information presented in this book.

While every effort has been made to ensure the accuracy of the information contained within this book, the author and publisher make no warranties or representations express or implied, about the completeness, accuracy, reliability, suitability, or availability with respect to the contents of this book for any purpose. The use of any information provided in this book is at the reader's own risk.

TABLE OF CONTENTS

INTRODUCTION: WELCOME TO YOUR READING ADVENTURE!

(Pg:3-5)

- Welcome to Your Reading Adventure!
- How to Use This Book
- Each story is designed to
- How to Use This Book
- A Note for Parents and Teachers

SECTION 1: FICTION STORIES

CHAPTER 1: ADVENTURE STORIES

(Pg:6-21)

Story Time: The Magic Compass

- Question Time: Reading Comprehension Exercise
- Answers

Story Time: The Lost City of Zephyr

- Question Time: Reading Comprehension Exercise
- Answers

CHAPTER 2: FAMILY & FRIENDSHIP

(Pg:22-34)

Story Time: The Treehouse Secret

- Question Time: Reading Comprehension Exercise
- Answers

Story Time: The New Kid

- Question Time: Reading Comprehension Exercise
- Answers

TABLE OF CONTENTS

CHAPTER 3: FANTASY & MAGIC (Pg:35 -48)

Story Time: Midnight's Magical Return

- Question Time: Reading Comprehension Exercise
- Answers

Story Time: Finn the Unlikely Hero

- Question Time: Reading Comprehension Exercise
- Answers

SECTION 2: NON-FICTION PASSAGES

CHAPTER 4: SCIENCE & NATURE (Pg:49 -59)

Passage: The Life of a Honeybee

- Question Time: Reading Comprehension Exercise
- Answers

Passage: Exploring the Rainforest

- Question Time: Reading Comprehension Exercise
- Answers

CHAPTER 5: HISTORY & CULTURE (Pg:60-70)

Passage: The History of the Olympics

- Question Time: Reading Comprehension Exercise
- Answers

Passage: The Story of Rosa Park

- Question Time: Reading Comprehension Exercise
- Answers

TABLE OF CONTENTS

SECTION 3: SOCIAL-EMOTIONAL LEARNING (SEL)

CHAPTER 6: EMPATHY & INCLUSION (Pg: 71-82)

PASSAGE: THE KINDNESS PROJECT

- Question Time: Reading Comprehension Exercise
- Answers

PASSAGE: THE BIG DECISION

- Question Time: Reading Comprehension Exercise
- Answers

SECTION 4: VOCABULARY BUILDERS

CHAPTER 7: CONTEXT CLUES & WORD MEANINGS (Pg: 83-90)

- Definition Clues
- Synonym Clues
- Antonym (Contrast) Clues
- Example Clues

SECTION 5: COMPREHENSION PRACTICE & ANSWER KEYS

CHAPTER 8: COMPREHENSION QUESTIONS (Pg: 91-100)

- Short Story (Fiction)
- Informational Text (Nonfiction)
- Poem
- Dialogue (Play Script)

Conclusion (Pg: 101-102)

Appendix Tables (Pg: 103-104)

- Common Reading Comprehension Question Starters
- Signal Words for Text Structures
- Context Clue Types and Clue Words
- Vocabulary Builder – Words for Comprehension

Introduction: Welcome to Your Reading Adventure!

Welcome to Your Reading Adventure!

Dear Reader,

Welcome to your 4th Grade Reading Comprehension Workbook! This book is your ticket to an exciting journey filled with adventure, mystery, discovery, and fun. Whether you're reading at home, in the classroom, or preparing for a big test, this workbook is here to help you become a confident, fluent, and thoughtful reader.

What's Inside?

This workbook is packed with 30 high-interest stories and passages that will keep you hooked from start to finish. You'll explore:

- **Fiction Stories:** Dive into magical worlds, solve mysteries, and meet unforgettable characters.
- **Nonfiction Passages:** Learn fascinating facts about science, history, nature, and more.
- **Social-Emotional Themes:** Discover stories that help you understand yourself and others better.

Each story is designed to:

- Build your reading fluency (so you can read faster and smoother).
- Expand your vocabulary (so you can learn new words and use them like a pro).
- Sharpen your critical thinking skills (so you can analyze, predict, and solve problems).

How to Use This Book

1. **Read at Your Own Pace**: You don't have to finish everything in one sitting. Take your time and enjoy each story!
2. **Answer the Questions**: After each story, you'll find multiple-choice and open-ended questions to test your understanding and spark your imagination.
3. **Learn New Words**: Look out for bolded vocabulary words and their definitions. Try using them in your own sentences!
4. **Track Your Progress**: Use the reading logs at the back of the book to celebrate how much you've accomplished.

A Note for Parents and Teachers

This workbook is more than just a reading tool—it's a way to help your child or student grow as a reader and thinker. Here's how you can support them:

- **Encourage curiosity**: Ask them about the stories and what they learned.
- **Celebrate progress**: Praise their efforts and improvements, no matter how small.
- **Make it fun:** Turn reading into a shared adventure by discussing the stories together.

Let's Get Started!

Are you ready to explore new worlds, solve puzzles, and uncover hidden treasures? Grab a pencil, find a cozy spot, and let's begin your reading adventure. Remember, every page you read brings you one step closer to becoming a super reader!

SECTION 1: FICTION STORIES

Chapter 1: Adventure Stories

Chapter 1: Adventure Stories

Objective: Engage students with imaginative stories that promote creativity, critical thinking, and empathy.

Story Time: The Magic Compass

One sunny afternoon, Mia and Jake were exploring their grandparents' attic when they stumbled upon an old, dusty box. Inside was a strange-looking compass with glowing symbols. As soon as Mia touched it, the compass began to spin wildly, and a map appeared in the air!

The map showed a path to a hidden treasure in the nearby Whispering Woods. But there was a warning: *"Only those who work together and never give up will succeed."*

Excited, Mia and Jake packed their backpacks and set off. As they entered the woods, they heard a faint whimpering sound. Following the noise, they found a small, scruffy dog with a muddy paw stuck under a rock. Mia and Jake carefully freed the dog, who wagged his tail gratefully.

"Let's call him Scout," Jake said, patting the dog's head. Scout barked happily and trotted alongside them as they continued their journey.

Their first challenge was a **rickety bridge** over a rushing river. Mia and Jake worked together to steady the bridge while Scout bravely led the way, sniffing out the safest path.

Next, they faced a ***maze of thorny bushes***. Just as they were about to give up, Scout sniffed the ground and found a hidden trail. He barked excitedly, guiding them through the maze without a single scratch.

Finally, they reached a giant tree with a ***mysterious riddle*** carved into its bark:I speak without a mouth and hear without ears. I have no body, but I come alive with the wind. What am I?"

Mia and Jake thought hard, but Scout barked at a nearby echo, giving them the clue they needed. "An echo!" they shouted together.

The tree creaked open, revealing a chest filled with ancient books and a note that read: ***"The real treasure is the journey and the friends you make along the way."***

Mia, Jake, and Scout returned home, tired but happy. They knew they had found not just a treasure, but a lifelong friend in Scout.

QUESTION TIME

1. What did Mia and Jake find in the attic?
   - a) A toy car
   - b) A magic compass
   - c) A photo album
   - d) A pair of shoes

2. What was the warning on the map?
   - a) "Turn back now!"
   - b) "Only those who work together and never give up will succeed."
   - c) "Beware of the dragon."
   - d) "The treasure is fake."

3. Who helped Mia and Jake through the maze of thorny bushes?
   - a) A bird
   - b) A cat
   - c) Scout the dog
   - d) A squirrel

VOCABULARY MATCH THE FOLLOWING

Column A	Column B
1. Compass	a) A puzzle or question that needs solving
2. Whimpering	b) A tool that shows direction

3. Riddle	c) A soft crying sound
4. Ancient	d) Very old
5. Treasure	e) Valuable items hidden or stored

TRUE OR FALSE

1. Mia and Jake found the compass in their grandparents' basement.
2. Scout helped them cross the rickety bridge.
3. The treasure chest was filled with gold coins.
4. The riddle was carved into a giant tree.
5. The note in the chest said, "The real treasure is the journey."

ARRANGE IN ORDER

Arrange these events in the correct sequence:
a) Mia and Jake freed Scout from under a rock.
b) They solved the riddle and found the treasure.
c) They found a magic compass in the attic.
d) Scout helped them navigate the maze of thorny bushes.
e) They crossed the rickety bridge over the river.

SHORT ANSWER QUESTIONS

1. What did Scout do to help Mia and Jake in the maze?
2. What was the riddle, and what was the answer?
3. What did the note in the treasure chest say, and what do you think it means?

ANSWERS

QUESTION TIME

- b) A magic compass
- b) "Only those who work together and never give up will succeed."
- c) Scout the dog

VOCABULARY MATCH THE FOLLOWING

Column A	Column B
1. Compass	b) A tool that shows direction
2. Whimpering	c) A soft crying sound
3. Riddle	a) A puzzle or question that needs solving
4. Ancient	d) Very old
5. Treasure	e) Valuable items hidden or stored

TRUE OR FALSE

1. False
2. True
3. False
4. True
5. True

ARRANGE IN ORDER

Correct Order: c, a, e, d, b

SHORT ANSWER QUESTIONS

1. Scout sniffed the ground and found a hidden trail, guiding them safely through the maze.
2. The riddle was: "I speak without a mouth and hear without ears. I have no body, but I come alive with the wind. What am I?" The answer was an echo.
3. The note said, "The real treasure is the journey and the friends you make along the way." It means that the experiences and friendships we gain are more valuable than material treasures.

Story Time: The Lost City of Zephyr

Emma loved reading about ancient civilizations, so when her teacher announced a field trip to the desert to explore the ruins of Zephyr, she was thrilled! Zephyr was a legendary city said to have been filled with gold and advanced technology, but it had vanished centuries ago.

On the trip, Emma and her classmate Liam wandered away from the group, curious to explore on their own. As they climbed over a rocky hill, they stumbled upon a hidden entrance to an underground tunnel. Inside, the walls glowed with strange symbols, and a faint hum filled the air.

"This is amazing!" Liam whispered, his flashlight bouncing off the glowing walls.

Emma noticed a map etched into the stone floor. It showed a path to the heart of the city. "Let's follow it!" she said, her eyes sparkling with excitement.

Their first challenge was a **room filled with mirrors**. The reflections were so confusing that Emma and Liam couldn't tell which way was real. "We need to think carefully," Emma said. They used a piece of chalk to mark the walls, finally finding the exit.

Next, they faced a **locked door with a puzzle**. The symbols on the door matched the ones on the walls. Emma remembered a book she'd read about ancient codes. "I think this symbol means 'knowledge,'" she said, pointing to a glowing shape. Together, they deciphered the code and unlocked the door.

Finally, they reached a **narrow ledge** over a deep pit. Liam hesitated, but Emma encouraged him. "We've come this far. We can't give up now!" They held hands and carefully crossed the ledge, their hearts pounding.

At the end of the tunnel, they found a chamber filled with ancient artifacts: golden statues, strange machines, and scrolls covered in writing. In the center of the room was a pedestal with a glowing message: **"The greatest treasure is knowledge."**

Emma and Liam smiled. They knew they had discovered something far more valuable than gold.

QUESTION TIME

1. What did Emma and Liam find in the underground tunnel?
   - a) A treasure chest
   - b) Glowing walls and a map
   - c) A dragon
   - d) A time machine

2. What was the first challenge Emma and Liam faced?
   - a) A locked door with a puzzle
   - b) A room filled with mirrors
   - c) A narrow ledge over a deep pit
   - d) A maze of thorny bushes

3. What did the message in the chamber say?
   - a) "Gold is the greatest treasure."
   - b) "The greatest treasure is knowledge."
   - c) "Beware of the curse."
   - d) "Leave and never return."

VOCABULARY MATCH THE FOLLOWING

Column A	Column B
1. Artifact	a) very old
2. Legend	b) An object made by humans, especially from long ago

3. Decipher	c) A story from the past that may or may not be true
4. Pedestal	d) To solve or interpret something difficult
5. Ancient	e) A base or support for a statue or object

TRUE OR FALSE

1. Emma and Liam found the entrance to the tunnel while exploring with the whole class.
2. The room filled with mirrors was easy to navigate.
3. Emma used her knowledge of ancient codes to solve the puzzle on the locked door.
4. The chamber at the end of the tunnel was filled with gold coins.
5. The message in the chamber said, "The greatest treasure is knowledge."

ARRANGE IN ORDER

Arrange these events in the correct sequence:

a) Emma and Liam deciphered the code on the locked door.
b) They found a chamber filled with artifacts and a glowing message.
c) They entered a room filled with confusing mirrors.
d) Emma and Liam discovered a hidden entrance to an underground tunnel.
e) They crossed a narrow ledge over a deep pit.

SHORT ANSWER QUESTIONS

1. What did Emma and Liam use to mark the walls in the mirror room?
2. How did Emma and Liam solve the puzzle on the locked door?
3. What do you think the message "The greatest treasure is knowledge" means?

ANSWERS
QUESTION TIME

1. b) Glowing walls and a map
2. b) A room filled with mirrors
3. b) "The greatest treasure is knowledge."

VOCABULARY MATCH THE FOLLOWING

Column A	Column B
1. Artifact	b) An object made by humans, especially from long ago
2. Legend	c) A story from the past that may or may not be true
3. Decipher	d) To solve or interpret something difficult
4. Pedestal	e) A base or support for a statue or object
5. Ancient	a) Very old

TRUE OR FALSE

1. False
2. False
3. True
4. False
5. True

ARRANGE IN ORDER

Correct Order: d, c, a, e, b

SHORT ANSWER QUESTIONS

1. Emma and Liam used a piece of chalk to mark the walls in the mirror room.
2. Emma remembered a book she'd read about ancient codes and deciphered the symbols on the door.
3. The message means that knowledge and learning are more valuable than material treasures like gold.

Chapter 2 : Family & Friendship

Chapter 2 : Family & Friendship

Objective: Explore themes of trust, loyalty, empathy, and inclusion through relatable stories that strengthen family bonds and friendships.

Story Time: The Treehouse Secret

Sophia and her little brother Max had always been close, but lately, Max had been acting strange. He would disappear for hours, and when Sophia asked where he'd been, he'd just say, "It's a secret."

One afternoon, Sophia noticed Max sneaking into the old treehouse in their backyard. Curious, she followed him. Inside, she found Max sitting with a notebook, scribbling furiously. Their cousin Jake was there too, drawing pictures on a large sheet of paper.

"What are you two doing?" Sophia asked, raising an eyebrow.

Max hesitated, then said, "Promise you won't tell anyone?"

Sophia nodded, and Max confided in her. He and Jake were working on a surprise for their parents' anniversary—a storybook about their family.

In the story, they were superheroes who saved the world together. "We wanted it to be special," Max explained.

Sophia's heart melted. "That's amazing! Let me help you."

Together, the three of them worked on the story, adding illustrations, creating a comic strip, and even designing a cover. When they presented it to their parents on their anniversary, their mom cried happy tears, and their dad said, "This is the best gift we've ever received."

From that day on, Sophia, Max, and Jake had a new bond—a shared secret that made their family relationship even stronger.

READING COMPREHENSION QUESTIONS

Directions: Answer the questions based on the story.

1. Why was Sophia curious about Max's behavior?
2. Where did Sophia follow Max to?
3. What were Max and Jake working on?
4. What was the storybook about?
5. How did the parents react to the gift?

VOCABULARY MATCH THE FOLLOWING

Directions: Match each word to its correct meaning.

Word	Meaning
1. Confided	A. Drew quickly and roughly
2. Scribbling	B. Shared a secret
3. Hesitated	C. Paused before speaking
4. Curious	D. Wanting to know something
5. Anniversary	E. Yearly celebration of an event

FILL IN THE BLANKS

Directions: Complete the sentences using words from the box.

(**Word Box:** treehouse, secret, superheroes, notebook, anniversary)

1. Max and Jake were working on a surprise for their parents' _____.
2. Sophia found Max scribbling in a _____ in the _____.
3. The storybook was about their family as _____.
4. Max didn't want to tell Sophia at first because it was a _____.

TRUE OR FALSE

Directions: Write T (True) or F (False).

1. Sophia was angry when she found Max in the treehouse.
2. The storybook was about aliens invading Earth.
3. Jake helped Max with the surprise.
4. Their dad didn't like the gift.
5. The secret brought the kids closer together.

SEQUENCE THE EVENTS

Directions: Number the events from 1-5 in the correct order.

____ Sophia followed Max to the treehouse.
____ Their parents loved the gift.
____ Max kept saying, "It's a secret."
____ Sophia helped finish the storybook.
____ Max and Jake worked on a family superhero story.

ANSWERS

READING COMPREHENSION

- Because Max kept disappearing and saying, "It's a secret."
- The old treehouse in their backyard.
- A surprise storybook for their parents' anniversary.
- Their family as superheroes saving the world.
- Their mom cried happy tears, and their dad said it was the best gift ever.

VOCABULARY MATCH

1-B, 2-A, 3-C, 4-D, 5-E

FILL IN THE BLANKS ANSWERS

1. anniversary
2. notebook / treehouse
3. superheroes
4. secret

TRUE OR FALSE ANSWERS

1-F, 2-F, 3-T, 4-F, 5-T

SEQUENCE THE EVENTS ANSWERS

1. Max kept saying, "It's a secret."
2. Sophia followed Max to the treehouse.
3. Max and Jake worked on a family superhero story.
4. Sophia helped finish the storybook.
5. Their parents loved the gift.

Story Time: The New Kid

When a new student named Amir joined Mia's class, everyone was curious. Amir wore different clothes, spoke with an accent, and brought strange-looking food for lunch. Some kids whispered behind his back, and others avoided him altogether.

Mia noticed Amir sitting alone at lunch and remembered how she felt when she was new to the school. She decided to sit with him.

"Hi, I'm Mia," she said with a smile. Amir looked surprised but smiled back. "I'm Amir. Thanks for sitting with me."

As they talked, Mia learned that Amir was from Syria and loved soccer. She invited him to join her friends at recess, and soon, Amir was playing soccer with everyone.

One day, a group of kids made fun of Amir's lunch. Mia's best friend, Lily, joined in the teasing. Mia felt torn—she didn't want to upset Lily, but she knew it was wrong to treat Amir that way.

She stood up for him. "His food might look different, but it's delicious. You should try it before judging."

Amir smiled gratefully. "Thanks, Mia. You're a true friend." Later, Mia talked to Lily about how her actions hurt Amir.

Lily apologized and even tried some of Amir's food the next day. By the end of the week, Amir wasn't the "new kid" anymore—he was just another friend in the class, thanks to Mia's kindness and inclusion.

READING COMPREHENSION (MULTIPLE CHOICE)

(1) Why did Mia decide to sit with Amir at lunch?
- a) She felt sorry for him.
- b) She remembered how it felt to be new.
- c) She wanted to impress her friends.
- d) She was curious about his food.

(2) What did Mia do when kids made fun of Amir's lunch?
- a) She ignored them.
- b) She joined in the teasing.
- c) She stood up for him.
- d) She told the teacher.

VOCABULARY MATCH

Directions: Match each word to its definition.

Word	Definition
1. Exclude	A. Welcoming someone for who they are.
2. Acceptance	B. Differences among people.
3. Diversity	C. To leave someone out.

FILL IN THE BLANKS

Directions: Complete the sentences.

1. Mia sat with Amir at lunch because she remembered how it felt to be _____.
2. Amir's lunch looked different because he was from _____.
3. Mia's friend _____ teased Amir at first but later apologized.

TRUE OR FALSE

Directions: Write T (True) or F (False).

1. Amir was from Canada.
2. Mia stood up for Amir when others laughed at his food.
3. Lily never apologized to Amir.

ANSWERS

MULTIPLE CHOICE ANSWERS

- b) She remembered how it felt to be new.
- c) She stood up for him.

VOCABULARY MATCH ANSWERS

1-C, 2-A, 3-B

TRUE OR FALSE ANSWERS

1. F
2. T
3. F

FILL IN THE BLANKS ANSWERS

1. new
2. Syria
3. Lily

Chapter 3. Fantasy & Magic

Chapter 3 : Fantasy & Magic

Objective: Spark imagination while teaching bravery, responsibility, and problem-solving through magical adventures with surprising twists!

Story Time: Midnight's Magical Return

Lily had loved her shiny black cat Midnight more than anything. When he disappeared three summers ago, she left his favorite red collar hanging on her bedpost, hoping he'd come back.

One drizzly Tuesday after school, Lily spotted something impossible near the old oak tree—glowing blue pawprints in the shape of Midnight's big furry feet! Her heart pounded as she followed them into the woods, her rain boots splashing through puddles that tinkled like windchimes.

Under the twisty oak, the air smelled suddenly of Midnight's favorite treats—tuna and catnip. Then she heard it:
"Mrrow?"

Midnight sat on a mossy rock, his fur dotted with twinkling stardust, wearing his red collar! He leapt into Lily's arms, purring so hard his whole body vibrated.

Thorn, the grumpy badger who guarded the forest, shuffled out from behind a mushroom.

"Your cat's been keeping our magic safe," he muttered. "But he meowed about you every night."

As Lily cuddled Midnight, his collar glowed bright blue—the same color as the magical pawprints. Now she'd always be able to find him, no matter what.

That night, as Lily fell asleep, Midnight kneaded his paws against her pillow just like old times.

Outside, the oak tree's leaves shimmered silver, whispering secrets only happy endings know.

MULTIPLE CHOICE

Directions: Answer the questions based on the story.

1) What guided Lily to the magical oak tree?
a) Glowing blue pawprints
b) Singing birds
c) A trail of candy
d) Floating lanterns

2) What was special about Midnight's collar?
a) It played music
b) It glowed when magic was near
c) It could turn invisible
d) It changed colors daily

3) How did Thorn the badger feel about Lily at first?
a) Excited
b) Grumpy
c) Scared
d) Bored

TRUE/FALSE

1) The magical pawprints led Lily to a river. (T/F)

2) Midnight had been living as a fox in the forest. (T/F)

3) Lily's raincoat was purple. (T/F)

VOCABULARY

1) Which word describes how the puddles sounded?

a) Crunchy
b) Tinkling
c) Roaring
d) Hissing

2) What does "bioluminescent" mean?

a) Glowing naturally
b) Extremely old
c) Covered in moss
d) Very smelly

3) Midnight's fur was dotted with:

a) Mud
b) Stardust
c) Sand
d) Flower petals

SEQUENCE THE EVENTS

Directions: Number the events in the correct order.

1) Number these events:
___ Thorn explains Midnight's secret
___ Lily touches the oak tree
___ Midnight kneads the pillow

2) Number these events:
   ___ Lily sees glowing prints
   ___ The collar begins to glow
   ___ Raindrops hang magically

3) Number these events:
   ___ Midnight purrs in Lily's arms
   ___ Lily's boots splash in puddles
   ___ Badger adjusts his glasses

SHORT ANSWER

1) Why did the oak tree whisper to Lily?

2) How did Lily know the blue fox was really Midnight?

3) What lesson did Lily learn from her adventure?

ANSWERS

MULTIPLE CHOICE

1. a) Glowing blue pawprints
2. b) It glowed when magic was near
3. b) Grumpy

TRUE/FALSE

1. False
2. False
3. False

VOCABULARY

1. b) Tinkling
2. a) Glowing naturally
3. b) Stardust

SEQUENCE THE EVENTS

1.) 2, 1, 3
2.) 1, 3, 2
3.) 3, 1, 2

SHORT ANSWER

1. It recognized her loyalty/love for Midnight
2. Recognized his green eyes and collar
3. Answers vary: "True friendship lasts"/"Magic is real" etc.

Story Time: Finn the Unlikely Hero

Finn wiped sweat from his forehead as another spell fizzled in his hands. At Stormhaven Magic School, everyone could do magic... except him.

Yesterday's Disaster:

His "flower-growing" spell turned Headmaster Grumblewort's beard into hissing snakes! The school laughed—especially Vex, the smirking bully who called him "Finn the Flop."

The Big Test:

On Annual Magic Day, students paired up for challenges. Finn's stomach dropped when he saw his partner—Vex!

First Challenge: Fix the Broken Bridge
Vex whispered a forbidden shadow spell.
FINN: "Stop! That's dangerous!"
BOOM! The spell backfired, causing:

🪶 Spells to fly backward
🐉 Magical creatures to escape
🏰 School towers to crumble

The Surprise:

A glowing ghost appeared—Founder Wispwillow, who built the school! "Chaos isn't a curse," he said. "It's a test! Only those who fix mistakes can stop it."

Finn's Brave Moment:

He turned to Vex. "Help me?"
Together, they used Finn's "failed" spells in new ways:
💀 His snake spell became rescue ropes
💥 His exploding orbs stunned runaway creatures
🌈 His color-changing trick calmed the magic storm

When the last tower stabilized, the crowd erupted. Even Vex grinned. "Not bad, Finn."
Founder Wispwillow winked. "The best magic comes from second tries."
Now, Finn wasn't "the Flop"—he was Finn the Fixer!

READING COMPREHENSION (MULTIPLE CHOICE)

(1) What was Finn's nickname at school?
- a) Finn the Flash
- b) Finn the Flop
- c) Finn the Fast

(2) What appeared when the spells backfired?
- a) A dragon
- b) Founder Wispwillow's ghost
- c) A rainbow.

(3) How did Finn's snake spell help?
- a) Made ropes to save towers
- b) Fed the escaped creatures
- c) Cleaned the classrooms

TRUE/FALSE

- Vex was happy to be Finn's partner at first. (T/F)
- The chaos was actually a planned test. (T/F)
- Finn fixed everything alone. (T/F)

VOCABULARY

1) Which word means "a big failure"?

- a) Fizzled
- b) Disaster
- c) Whispered

2) What does "forbidden" mean?
- a) Not allowed
- b) Very powerful
- c) Brand new

3) "Stabilized" means:
- a) Fell apart
- b) Became steady
- c) Disappeared

SEQUENCING

- **Number these:**
1. ____ Spells backfire
2. ____ Ghost appears
3. ____ Finn partners with Vex

- **Number these:**
1. ____ Towers crumble
2. ____ Snake spell helps
3. ____ Annual Magic Day starts

SHORT ANSWER

1) Why was Finn's magic useful in the end?

2) What lesson did Vex learn?

3) How did Finn prove he wasn't a "flop"?

ANSWERS

MULTIPLE CHOICE ANSWERS

1. b) Finn the Flop
2. b) Founder's ghost
3. a) Made ropes

TRUE/FALSE

1. False
2. True
3. False

VOCABULARY

1. b) Disaster
2. a) Not allowed
3. b) Became steady

SEQUENCING

- 2, 3, 1
- 3, 1, 2

SHORT ANSWER

1. His "failed" spells had new uses
2. Teamwork matters / Don't bully
3. Fixed the chaos / Became "Finn the Fixer"

SECTION 2 : NON FICTION PASSAGES

Chapter 4: Science & Nature

Objective: Build knowledge and comprehension through informative, real-world topics.

Passage : The Life of a Honeybee

Bees are tiny but mighty insects that play a big role in nature. They live together in large groups called colonies. A colony has one queen bee, many worker bees (females), and some drone bees (males). Each bee has a special job to help the colony survive.

Ecosystems and Bees

Bees are important for ecosystems, communities of living things and their environment. They help plants grow by pollination, which is when pollen moves from one flower to another. This helps plants make fruits and seeds. Without bees, many plants would not grow, and animals that eat those plants would struggle to survive.

Pollination: How Bees Help Plants

When a bee lands on a flower to drink nectar, pollen sticks to its legs and body. As the bee flies to the next flower, some pollen falls off, helping the plant reproduce. Many foods we eat, like apples, strawberries, and almonds, depend on bees for pollination.

Why Bees Are in Danger

Sadly, bees face many threats, such as pesticides (chemicals that kill insects), loss of flowers, and diseases. If bees disappear, our food supply could be in trouble. People can help bees by planting flowers, avoiding harmful chemicals, and building bee-friendly gardens.

Vocabulary

1. Colony – A group of bees living together.
2. Pollinate – To move pollen from one flower to another, helping plants grow.
3. Ecosystem – A community of living things and their environment.

COMPREHENSION EXERCISES

A. Fact Recall (Answer in complete sentences)

1. What are the three types of bees in a colony?
2. How do bees help plants grow?
3. Name one threat to honeybees.

B. Cause and Effect (Explain the relationship)

1. What happens if bees do not pollinate flowers?
2. Why do some farmers depend on bees?
3. How can people help protect bees?

C. Critical Thinking (Short answers)

1. Why are bees important to humans?
2. How would the ecosystem change if bees disappeared?
3. What is one way your school could help bees?

FILL IN THE BLANKS

1) Bees live together in a group called a _____. (colony / ecosystem)

2) When bees move pollen from flower to flower, it is called _____. (pollination / threat)

3) Many foods like apples and almonds need _____ to grow. (pesticides / bees)

TRUE OR FALSE

Instructions: Write T for True or F for False.

1. Worker bees are all male. (_)
2. Bees help plants by carrying pollen. (_)
3. Pesticides are helpful to bees and do not harm them. (_)

ANSWERS

COMPREHENSION EXERCISES

A. Fact Recall
1. The three types of bees are the queen bee, worker bees, and drone bees.
2. Bees help plants grow by carrying pollen from one flower to another.
3. One threat to honeybees is pesticides.

B. Cause and Effect
1. If bees do not pollinate flowers, many plants will not grow fruits or seeds.
2. Farmers depend on bees because they help crops like apples and almonds grow.
3. People can help bees by planting flowers and avoiding harmful chemicals.

C. Critical Thinking
1. Bees are important to humans because they help grow food we eat.
2. If bees disappeared, many plants would die, and animals that eat those plants would struggle.
3. My school could help bees by planting a garden with bee-friendly flowers.

FILL IN THE BLANKS

1. Bees live together in a group called a colony.
2. When bees move pollen from flower to flower, it is called pollination.
3. Many foods like apples and almonds need bees to grow.

TRUE OR FALSE

1. Worker bees are all male. (F) (Worker bees are female.)
2. Bees help plants by carrying pollen. (T)
3. Pesticides are helpful to bees and do not harm them. (F) (Pesticides can harm bees.)

Passage: Exploring the Rainforest

Rainforests are some of the most amazing places on Earth! They are thick, green forests that receive lots of rain all year round. These forests are home to millions of plants and animals, many of which cannot be found elsewhere.

Biodiversity: Nature's Treasure

Rainforests have incredible biodiversity, which means they are full of many different kinds of life. You might find colorful birds, monkeys swinging from trees, and thousands of insects in just one small area. Scientists believe that more than half of the world's plant and animal species live in rainforests!

Layers of the Rainforest

Rainforests have different layers, like a tall green cake. The tallest layer is called the canopy, where the tops of the trees form a leafy roof. Below the canopy is the understory, where smaller plants and young trees grow. The forest floor is the darkest and dampest layer, where decomposers like fungi break down dead plants and animals.

Conservation: Protecting Rainforests

Sadly, rainforests are in danger. Many trees are cut down for wood, farming, and roads. When this happens, animals lose their homes, and some become endangered, meaning they might disappear forever. People can help protect rainforests by recycling, using less paper, and supporting conservation efforts.

COMPREHENSION EXERCISES

A. Main Idea & Supporting Details (Answer in complete sentences)

1. What is the main idea of this passage?
2. Name two facts that support why rainforests are important.
3. What is one way people can help protect rainforests?

B. Inferencing (Use clues from the text to answer)

1. Why do you think the forest floor is dark and damp?
2. How might cutting down trees affect animals in the rainforest?
3. Why do scientists study rainforests?

FILL IN THE BLANKS

1. The top layer of the rainforest is called the _____. (canopy / understory)
2. When a species is at risk of disappearing, it is _____. (endangered / biodiversity)
3. Rainforests have high _____ because they have so many different plants and animals. (conservation / biodiversity)

TRUE OR FALSE

1. Rainforests only have one layer where all animals live. (_)
2. Many medicines come from rainforest plants. (_)
3. Cutting down trees has no effect on rainforest animals. (_)

MATCH THE WORD TO ITS MEANING

Definition Options	Definition Options
Biodiversity	A. Protecting nature from harm
Canopy	B. The top layer of trees in a rainforest
Endangered	B. The top layer of trees in a rainforest
Ecosystem	D. The variety of life in an area
Pollinate	E. A community of living things and their environment
Conservation	F. At risk of disappearing forever

ANSWERS

COMPREHENSION EXERCISES

A. Main Idea & Supporting Details
1. The main idea is that rainforests are important ecosystems with rich biodiversity, but they need protection.
2. Rainforests are home to more than half of the world's species. (2) They provide oxygen and medicines.
3. People can help by recycling and using less paper.

B. Inferencing
1. The forest floor is dark and damp because the thick canopy blocks sunlight.
2. Cutting down trees destroys animal habitats, leaving them with no food or shelter.
3. Scientists study rainforests to learn about rare species and discover new medicines.

FILL IN THE BLANKS

1. The top layer of the rainforest is called the canopy.
2. When a species is at risk of disappearing, it is endangered.
3. Rainforests have high biodiversity because they have so many different plants and animals.

TRUE OR FALSE

1. Rainforests only have one layer where all animals live. (F) (Rainforests have multiple layers.)
2. Many medicines come from rainforest plants. (T)
3. Cutting down trees has no effect on rainforest animals. (F) (It destroys their homes.)

MATCH THE FOLLOWING

Word	Word
Biodiversity	D
Canopy	B
Endangered	F
Ecosystem	E
Pollinate	C
Conservation	A

Chapter 5: History & Culture

Objective: Build reading comprehension skills while learning about the exciting history of the Olympics, from ancient times to today!

Passage: The History of the Olympics

Ancient Beginnings

The Olympics started over 2,700 years ago in Ancient Greece! The games were held in Olympia to honor Zeus, the king of the Greek gods. Unlike today, the ancient Olympics had only a few events, like running, wrestling, and chariot racing. Winners didn't get gold medals—they received olive wreaths as prizes!

The games were so important that wars would stop during the Olympics so athletes could travel safely. This was called the "Olympic Truce."

The Modern Olympics

After disappearing for centuries, the Olympics returned in 1896 in Athens, Greece. A Frenchman named Pierre de Coubertin helped bring them back. Now, athletes from all over the world compete in hundreds of sports, from swimming to gymnastics.

One big difference between ancient and modern Olympics? Women couldn't compete in ancient times, but today, female athletes win medals just like men!

Olympics Today: Bringing the World Together

The Olympics are about more than just sports—they celebrate peace, teamwork, and unity. A new host city welcomes athletes and fans from over 200 countries every four years. The opening ceremony is a huge show with music, dancing, and the lighting of the Olympic flame, a tradition that started in ancient Greece.

The Olympics teach us that we can compete fairly and respect each other regardless of our background.

COMPREHENSION EXERCISES

A. Chronological Order *(Number the events 1-4 in the order they happened.)*

___ The modern Olympics began in Athens.
___ Ancient Greeks held the first Olympics.
___ Women were allowed to compete.
___ Pierre de Coubertin helped restart the Olympics.

B. Compare & Contrast (Answer in complete sentences.)

1. How were the ancient Olympics different from the modern Olympics?
2. What is one way the ancient and modern Olympics are similar?
3. Why do you think the Olympics are important today?

C. Personal Reflection *(Write 2-3 sentences.)*

If you could compete in any Olympic sport, which would you choose and why?

FILL IN THE BLANKS

1. The Olympics are a _____ that started long ago. (tradition/competition)
2. Athletes show _____ by respecting each other. (unity/tradition)
3. Running and swimming are types of _____. (competition/unity)

TRUE OR FALSE

1. Ancient Olympic winners received gold medals. (T/F)
2. The Olympic Truce stopped wars during the games. (T/F)
3. Only men compete in the modern Olympics. (T/F)

OLYMPICS VOCABULARY MATCH

Draw a line to connect each word with its meaning:

Words
1. Tradition
2. Competition
3. Unity
4. Truce
5. Zeus
6. Athlete

Meanings

A. A contest between people or teams
B. Working together in peace
C. A custom passed down over time
D. The king of Greek gods
E. A pause in fighting for peace
F. Someone who trains for sports

ANSWERS

COMPREHENSION EXERCISES

A. Chronological Order
1. Ancient Greeks held the first Olympics.
2. Pierre de Coubertin helped restart the Olympics.
3. The modern Olympics began in Athens.
4. Women were allowed to compete.

B. Compare & Contrast
1. Ancient Olympics had fewer sports and only men competed.
2. Both have opening ceremonies and celebrate athletes.
3. They bring people together and promote peace.

C. Personal Reflection (Example answer)
"I would choose gymnastics because I love flipping and doing tricks. It looks fun and challenging!"

FILL IN THE BLANKS

1. tradition
2. unity
3. competition

TRUE OR FALSE

1. False (They got olive wreaths.)
2. True
3. False (Women compete too!)

VOCABULARY MATCH

1. Tradition → C
2. Competition → A
3. Unity → B
4. Truce → E
5. Zeus → D
6. Athlete → F

Passage: The Story of Rosa Park

"One Brave Act Changed History"

The Day Everything Changed

On December 1, 1955, in Montgomery, Alabama, a seamstress named Rosa Parks refused to give up her bus seat to a white passenger. This act defied segregation laws that kept Black and white people separate in public places, including buses.

Why It Mattered

Rosa wasn't just physically tired – she was tired of injustice. Her arrest sparked the Montgomery Bus Boycott, where Black citizens refused to ride city buses for 381 days. A young pastor named Dr. Martin Luther King Jr. emerged as a leader of this peaceful protest.

A Victory for Equality

In November 1956, the U.S. Supreme Court ruled that bus segregation was unconstitutional. This marked a major victory for the civil rights movement. Rosa Parks continued to work for justice and equality throughout her life, showing how one person's courage can help change the world.

Her Legacy Lives On

Rosa Parks is remembered as the "Mother of the Civil Rights Movement." Her bravery inspired millions to stand up against unfair treatment. Schools, streets, and libraries have been named in her honor. Every year, people celebrate her life and the change she helped bring. Rosa's story teaches us that standing up for what is right—even when you're standing alone—can lead to big, important change.

MULTIPLE CHOICE

1) Where did Rosa Parks' protest take place?
a) Birmingham, Alabama
b) Montgomery, Alabama
c) Atlanta, Georgia

2) How long did the Montgomery Bus Boycott last?
a) 100 days
b) 381 days
c) 1 year and 6 months

3) Who became a leader during the boycott?
a) Malcolm X
b) Dr. Martin Luther King Jr.
c) Thurgood Marshall

TRUE OR FALSE

1. Rosa Parks was a teacher.
2. The Supreme Court ruled bus segregation illegal in 1956.
3. Rosa Parks' protest happened because she was too tired to stand.

VOCABULARY MATCH

Match each word to its meaning:
1. Segregation
2. Boycott
3. Constitution

a) Refusing to use something as a protest
b) Separation by race
c) Supreme law of the U.S.

SHORT ANSWER

1. Ancient Olympic winners received gold medals. (T/F)
2. The Olympic Truce stopped wars during the games. (T/F)
3. Only men compete in the modern Olympics. (T/F)

CRITICAL THINKING

1. Why is Rosa called the "Mother of the Civil Rights Movement"?
2. How was Rosa's protest different from how superheroes fight injustice?
3. What lesson can students learn from Rosa's story?

ANSWERS

MULTIPLE CHOICE:

1. b) Montgomery, Alabama
2. b) 381 days
3. b) Dr. Martin Luther King Jr.

TRUE OR FALSE

1. False (she was a seamstress)
2. True
3. False (she was tired of unfair treatment)

VOCABULARY MATCH

1-b, 2-a, 3-c

SHORT ANSWER:

1. Seamstress
2. Schools/streets named after her, statues, holidays
3. It hurt bus companies financially

CRITICAL THINKING:

1. Her act inspired the movement
2. She used peaceful resistance, not violence
3. Answers vary (e.g., "One person can make a difference")

SECTION 3: SOCIAL-EMOTIONAL LEARNING (SEL)

Chapter 6: Empathy & Inclusion

Objective: Help students develop emotional intelligence and problem-solving skills through relatable stories.

Passage: The Kindness Project

Liam's fourth-grade class was buzzing with excitement. Their teacher, Ms. Rivera, had just announced The Kindness Project—a week-long challenge where students would work together to make their school a kinder place.

"Kindness isn't just about being nice," Ms. Rivera explained. "It's about noticing when someone needs help and taking initiative—that means stepping up without being asked."

Liam and his friends, Maya and Javier, brainstormed ideas. They noticed some kids sat alone at lunch or looked left out during recess. So, they decided their project would focus on inclusion, making sure everyone felt welcome.

A Plan for Kindness

1. Smile & Greet: Every morning, they stood by the classroom door, smiling and saying hello to every student.
2. Buddy Bench: At recess, they painted a bright bench where anyone could sit if they needed a friend.
3. Kindness Notes: They wrote encouraging messages and slipped them into classmates' desks.

At first, some students were shy, but soon, others joined in. Even the principal praised their collaboration—working together to make a difference.

By the end of the week, the whole school felt warmer. Liam realized kindness wasn't just a project—it was a habit that made everyone happier.

COMPREHENSION EXERCISES

1) **What was the main goal of The Kindness Project?**
a) To win a school competition
b) To make the school a kinder place
c) To paint the classroom
d) To learn new vocabulary words

2) **How did Liam's group decide to help others at recess?**
a) By giving out candy
b) By creating a Buddy Bench
c) By skipping recess
d) By playing only with their friends

TRUE OR FALSE

Write T for True or F for False.

1. The Kindness Project lasted for one day.
2. The students wrote encouraging notes to their classmates.
3. Only Liam worked on the project—no one else helped.

VOCABULARY MATCHING

Match each word to its meaning.

- Compassion
- Initiative
- Collaboration

a) Working together as a team
b) Caring about others' feelings
c) Taking the first step without being asked

SHORT ANSWER (CRITICAL THINKING)

1. Why do you think the Buddy Bench was a good idea?
2. How could you show kindness in your school?

SEQUENCING (STORY ORDER)

Number the events from 1 (first) to 3 (last).

___ They painted the Buddy Bench.
___ Ms. Rivera announced The Kindness Project.
___ Students wrote kindness notes for classmates.

FILL IN THE BLANKS

Use the word bank to complete the sentences:
(compassion, initiative, collaboration, Buddy Bench, inclusion)

1. Liam and his friends showed _____ by starting the project without being asked.
2. The _____ was painted bright yellow so no one would feel left out at recess.
3. The students practiced _____ when they worked together to write kindness notes.
4. Their project focused on _____, making sure everyone felt welcome.
5. Maya felt _____ when she saw a sad classmate and sat with them at lunch.

ANSWERS

COMPREHENSION EXERCISES

1. b
2. b

TRUE OR FALSE

1. False (They got olive wreaths.)
2. True
3. False (Women compete too!)

VOCABULARY MATCH

- Compassion: Answer: b) Caring about others' feelings
- Initiative : Answer: c) Taking the first step without being asked
- Collaboration: Answer: a) Working together as a team

SHORT ANSWER (CRITICAL THINKING)

1. It helped lonely kids find friends.
2. .Sit with someone who's alone at lunch.

SEQUENCING

1. Ms. Rivera announced The Kindness Project.
2. They painted the Buddy Bench.
3. Students wrote kindness notes for classmates.

FILL IN THE BLANKS

1. initiative
2. Buddy Bench
3. collaboration
4. inclusion
5. compassion

Passage: The Big Decision

"Ethan's Tough Choice"

The Day Everything Changed

Ethan had saved $40 to buy the new Falcon Force video game. He needed just $10 more to get it finally.

While helping clean up the classroom one afternoon, Ethan spotted something shiny under a desk — it was a $10 bill! His heart skipped a beat. But then he noticed tiny letters written on it: "Mia R."

Now, Ethan had a big decision to make.

The Dilemma:

Should he keep the money and buy the game today?

Or should he return it in case Mia needed it for something important?

He remembered what his teacher always said:

"Good choices build strong character."
Ethan quietly slipped the $10 into Mia's backpack.

The next day, Mia cheered when she found her lost lunch money. Ethan smiled — he felt proud, and that feeling was better than any video game.

At recess, Mia bought him a juice as a thank-you.

Ethan smiled, knowing he'd made the right decision.

MULTIPLE CHOICE

1) **Why was Ethan excited when he saw the $10 bill?**
   - a) He thought it belonged to the teacher
   - b) He could now buy his new game
   - c) He wanted to give it to Mia
   - d) He planned to buy lunch with it

2) **What made Ethan return the money instead of keeping it?**
   - a) He didn't want to carry cash
   - b) He remembered his teacher's words about good choices
   - c) He was afraid of getting caught
   - d) He already had enough money

3) **What did Ethan do with the $10 bill?**
   - a) He kept it
   - b) He gave it to the teacher
   - c) He put it in Mia's backpack
   - d) He threw it away

4) **How did Ethan feel after returning the money?**
   - a) Sad and angry
   - b) Proud and happy
   - c) Nervous and scared
   - d) Tired and hungry

5) **What can we learn from Ethan's story?**
   - a) Always buy what you want
   - b) Don't pick up money at school
   - c) Doing the right thing feels good
   - d) Games are more important than honesty

VOCABULARY MATCHING

Word	Definition
1. Dilemma	a) What happens because of your choice
2. Consequence	b) A hard choice between two options
3. Integrity	c) Doing what's right, even when it's difficult

GRAMMAR FIX – FIND THE MISTAKE

Each sentence below has one mistake. Circle it and write the correct word.

1. Ethan seen a $10 bill under the desk.
2. He feel nervous about what to do.
3. Mia cheer when she found her lunch money.

SENTENCE COMPLETION – CHOOSE THE BEST WORD

Choose the word that best completes each sentence.

1) A _____ is when you must choose between two difficult options.

a) game
b) dilemma
c) secret
d) plan

SENTENCE COMPLETION – CHOOSE THE BEST WORD

Choose the word that best completes each sentence.

2) The _____ of keeping the money might be feeling guilty.

- a) feeling
- b) decision
- c) consequence
- d) lesson

3) Ethan showed _____ by doing the honest thing.

- a) interest
- b) surprise
- c) excitement
- d) integrity

Please let us know how we're doing by leaving us a review.

 ANSWERS

READING COMPREHENSION

1. b
2. b
3. c
4. b
5. c

VOCABULARY MATCH

1. b
2. a
3. c

GRAMMAR FIX

- seen → saw
- feel → felt
- cheer → cheered

SENTENCE COMPLETION

1. b
2. c
3. d

SECTION 4: VOCABULARY BUILDERS

Chapter 7: Context Clues & Word Meanings

Objective:

Students will identify and utilize context clues to determine the meaning of unfamiliar words in texts.

Definition & Purpose

Context clues are hints within a sentence or paragraph that help readers decipher unknown words without a dictionary.

Types of Context Clues

Present with a guided notes table (students fill in examples during instruction):

- "When you see signal words like 'or' or 'but,' pause! They often introduce clues."

Type	Signal Words	Example Sentence	Inference
Definition	means, is, called	A biome, or natural environment, has unique plants.	biome = environment
Synonym	or, also known as	The castle was spacious (very roomy).	spacious = roomy
Contrast	but, unlike, however	Unlike the transparent glass, the wall was solid.	transparent = clear
Example	such as, including	Celestial bodies—like stars and planets—twinkle.	celestial = space-related

Examples

Definition Clues

The meaning is directly stated in the sentence.
Example 1:
"A herbivore, an animal that eats only plants, nibbled on leaves."
→ Clue: The phrase "an animal that eats only plants" defines herbivore.
Example 2:
"The castle had a moat, which is a deep ditch filled with water."
→ Clue: "Which is" signals the definition of moat.
Example 3:
"She studied geology, the science of rocks and Earth."
→ Clue: "The science of rocks and Earth" explains geology.

Synonym Clues

A similar word or phrase helps explain the unknown word.
Example 1:
"The puppy was exhausted, or completely tired, after playing."
→ Clue: "Or completely tired" restates exhausted.
Example 2:
"The path was arduous, very difficult, to climb."
→ Clue: "Very difficult" is a synonym for arduous.
Example 3:
"He felt furious—in other words, extremely angry."
→ Clue: "In other words" introduces the synonym angry.

Antonym (Contrast) Clues

An opposite word or phrase reveals the meaning.

Example 1:
"Unlike the tiny ant, the elephant was enormous."
➔ Clue: "Unlike" contrasts with enormous (so tiny = very small).

Example 2:
"The room was chaotic, not calm like usual."
➔ Clue: "Not calm" implies chaotic, meaning messy or wild.

Example 3:
"While Kyle was grumpy, his sister remained cheerful."
➔ Clue: "While" contrasts grumpy with cheerful (so grumpy = unhappy).

Example Clues

Examples help infer the word's meaning.

Example 1:
"Celestial bodies, such as stars and planets, glow at night."
➔ Clue: "Stars and planets" are examples of celestial things (so celestial = space-related).

Example 2:
"She loved pastries—donuts, muffins, and croissants."
➔ Clue: The list shows types of pastries (sweet baked goods).

Example 3:
"Precipitation, including rain, snow, and hail, fell all day."
➔ Clue: "Rain, snow, and hail" are forms of precipitation (weather water).

Inference Clues

You "read between the lines" using logic.

Example 1:
"She lurched forward when the bus stopped suddenly."
➔ Clue: Sudden bus stops make people jerk/move abruptly (lurched = moved suddenly).

Example 2:
"The parched soil cracked after months without rain."
➔ Clue: No rain → dry soil (parched = very dry).

Example 3:
"He gaped at the towering dinosaur skeleton."
➔ Clue: Towering skeletons surprise people (gaped = stared in shock).

IDENTIFY THE CLUE TYPE

Label each sentence with the type of context clue used (Definition, Synonym, Antonym, Example, Inference).

1. "A **paleontologist**, a scientist who studies fossils, found a dinosaur bone."
2. "The valley was **verdant**—lush and green—after the rain."
3. "Unlike the **frigid** poles, the equator is very hot."
4. "**Nocturnal** animals, like owls and bats, are active at night."
5. "She **flinched** as the loud firework exploded."

FILL IN THE BLANK

Choose the correct word using context clues.

1) "The snake moved _____, slithering silently through the grass."
   - a) clumsily
   - b) swiftly
   - c) stealthily

2) "The ancient vase was fragile—so _____ it could break easily."
   - a) heavy
   - b) delicate
   - c) colorful

3) "His generous act, like donating toys, showed he was _____."
   - a) selfish
   - b) kind
   - c) bored

INFERENCE CHALLENGE

Read the sentence and explain the bolded word's meaning in your own words.

1) "The **parched** soil cracked in the summer heat."
   → Parched means: _____

2) *"He **gaped** at the 10-foot-tall ice cream cone."*
   → Gaped means: _____

3) "The **dilapidated** house had broken windows and a sagging roof."
   → Dilapidated means: _____

CONTEXT CLUE DETECTIVE HUNT

Directions: Read each passage. I'd like for you to write the context clue, then write the meaning of the bolded word.

1) "The sapling, a young tree, bent in the wind."
   - Clue: _____
   - Sapling means: _____

2) "Unlike the crowded city, the village was peaceful and quiet."
   - Clue: _____
   - Crowded means: _____

3) "He was elated—so happy he jumped for joy!"
   - Clue: _____
   - Elated means: _____

 ANSWERS

IDENTIFY THE CLUE TYPE

1. Definition
2. Synonym
3. Antonym
4. Example
5. Inference

FILL IN THE BLANK

1. c) stealthily
2. b) delicate
3. b) kind

INFERENCE CHALLENGE

1. Parched = Very dry
2. Gaped = Stared in surprise
3. Dilapidated = Broken-down

CONTEXT CLUE DETECTIVE HUNT

1. Clue: "a young tree"
2. Sapling means: young tree
3. Clue: "Unlike... peaceful and quiet"
4. Crowded means: full of people/noisy
5. Clue: "so happy he jumped for joy"
6. Elated means: very happy

SECTION 5 : COMPREHENSION PRACTICE & ANSWER KEYS

Chapter 8 : Comprehension Questions

Comprehension Questions

1. Short Story (Fiction)

Title: "The Kindness Project" – Extended Version

Liam's class was buzzing with excitement. Their teacher, Mrs. Andrews, had announced Kindness Week—a whole week dedicated to spreading joy at school. Each student had to come up with an idea to make school a happier place.

Liam thought hard. One day, during lunch, he noticed a boy sitting alone. The next day, it was a different girl. That gave Liam an idea. He talked to his friends, and together they came up with the Buddy Bench—a special bench painted with bright colors. Anyone who felt lonely could sit on it, and others would know to come say hello or invite them to play.

They presented their idea to the principal and got permission to paint an old bench behind the library. By Friday, the Buddy Bench was already in place and working. One shy student, Maya, who had just moved to the school, sat on the bench. A group of kids saw her and invited her to play soccer. That day, Maya smiled more than she had all week.

Kindness Week ended, but the Buddy Bench stayed—and so did the friendships it started.

Questions:

1) What was the main idea of the story?

- a) Liam won a prize
- b) The kids had to do art projects
- c) Kindness can bring people together
- d) Maya started a new school

Comprehension Questions

2) Why did Liam want to create the Buddy Bench?

- a) His teacher told him to
- b) He wanted to decorate the playground
- c) He noticed some kids were lonely
- d) He wanted to be popular

3) What happened after they made the Buddy Bench?

- a) The teacher removed it
- b) Nobody used it
- c) Maya made new friends
- d) Liam sat alone

4) What character trait does Liam show?

- a) Selfishness
- b) Creativity
- c) Laziness
- d) Jealousy

5) What could be a good lesson from this story?

- a) Never play soccer alone
- b) Don't paint school benches
- c) Kindness makes school better
- d) Always eat lunch quickly

Informational Text (Nonfiction)

Title: "Polar Bears: Ice Kings" – Extended Version

Polar bears are large, powerful animals that live in the Arctic. They are well adapted to the cold. Their thick white fur blends in with the snow, and a thick layer of fat under their skin keeps them warm. They are excellent swimmers and can swim for hours in freezing water to hunt their favorite meal—seals.

These bears live on sea ice, where they wait by breathing holes to catch seals. But polar bears are now in danger. The Arctic is getting warmer, and the ice they rely on is melting earlier each year. This makes it harder for them to find food and travel across the ice.

Scientists around the world are studying polar bears to understand how climate change affects them. They also teach people about the small steps we can take, like saving energy or recycling, to protect the planet and help animals like polar bears.

Questions:

1) What helps polar bears stay warm in the cold Arctic?
- a) Drinking hot water
- b) Swimming all day
- c) Thick fur and fat
- d) Hiding in caves

2) What is the polar bear's favorite food?
1. a) Fish
2. b) Penguins
3. c) Seals
4. d) Walruses

3) Why are polar bears in danger?
1. a) People hunt them often
2. b) They have no food in summer
3. c) Melting ice is changing their habitat
4. d) Their fur is falling out

Informational Text (Nonfiction)

4) What can people do to help polar bears?

- a) Build new zoos
- b) Turn off unused lights
- c) Send them food
- d) Move them to warmer places

5) What is the main idea of this text?

- a) Polar bears love to eat seals
- b) Polar bears are in danger due to climate change
- c) Arctic ice is fun to play on
- d) Polar bears are dangerous animals

Poem

Title: "The Spring Dance" – Extended Version

The tulips twirl in dresses bright,
The robin sings with all his might.
The breeze hums soft—a gentle tune,
While clouds pirouette past the moon.
The grass wakes up, so fresh, so green,
The sun peeks out with golden sheen.
Children run with kites that fly,
While blossoms laugh beneath the sky.
Springtime whispers, "Come and play!"
And chases winter far away.

Questions:

1. What is the poem mostly about?

- a) Winter snowstorms
- b) Summer sports
- c) The beauty of spring
- d) A kite-flying contest

Poem

2) "Tulips twirl in dresses bright" is an example of:
- a) Simile
- b) Personification
- c) Alliteration
- d) Fact

3) What does the poet mean by "Springtime whispers"?
- a) Spring is loud
- b) Spring is quiet and gentle
- c) Spring is scary
- d) Spring shouts loudly

4) What is the mood of the poem?
- a) Angry and cold
- b) Sad and tired
- c) Joyful and playful
- d) Serious and dark

5) What do the clouds do in the poem?
- a) Make thunder
- b) Go to sleep
- c) Pirouette past the moon
- d) Rain heavily

Dialogue (Play Script)

"The Lost Lunch" – Extended Version

Mia: Oh no! My lunch money is gone!
Ethan: (holding a five-dollar bill) Is this yours? It says "Mia R." on it.
Mia: Yes! Thank you for being honest, Ethan.
Ethan: No problem. I found it by the swings.
Mia: You're the best. I was so worried. I was about to go tell the teacher.
Ethan: I'm just glad it wasn't lost forever.
Mia: Thanks to you, now I can still get my favorite—chicken nuggets and chocolate milk!

Dialogue (Play Script)

Questions:

1) What is Mia's problem at the beginning?
- a) She forgot her lunchbox
- b) She lost her money
- c) She is late for lunch
- d) She dropped her chocolate milk

2) How does Ethan help Mia?
- a) Gives her new money
- b) Shares his lunch
- c) Returns the money he found
- d) Buys her a snack

3) Where did Ethan find the money?
- a) In the lunchroom
- b) By the teacher's desk
- c) Under Mia's tray
- d) Near the swings

4) What can we learn about Ethan's character?
- a) He is sneaky
- b) He is honest
- c) He is silly
- d) He is forgetful

5) What is the tone of this script?
- a) Sad and scary
- b) Funny and confusing
- c) Friendly and thankful
- d) Angry and loud

Practical Text (Recipe)

Title: "Easy Peanut Butter Balls" – Extended Version

Ingredients:
- 1 cup peanut butter
- ½ cup honey
- 2 cups oats
- ½ teaspoon vanilla (optional)

Steps:
- In a big bowl, mix peanut butter and honey until smooth.
- Add oats and vanilla. Mix well.
- Roll the mixture into small balls.
- Place them on a tray and chill for 1 hour in the refrigerator.
- Enjoy as a healthy snack!

Questions:

1) What is the first step of the recipe?
   - a) Roll into balls
   - b) Mix peanut butter and honey
   - c) Chill for 1 hour
   - d) Add oats and vanilla

2) What is the purpose of chilling the balls?
   - a) To make them softer
   - b) To make them easier to eat
   - c) To help them hold their shape
   - d) To add flavor

3) Which ingredient is optional?
   - a) Oats
   - b) Honey
   - c) Vanilla
   - d) Peanut butter

4) How many cups of oats are needed?
   - a) 1 cup
   - b) 2 cups
   - c) ½ cup
   - d) 3 cups

5) What is the purpose of this text?
   - a) To tell a story
   - b) To give facts about oats
   - c) To explain how to make a snack
   - d) To describe peanut butter

 ANSWERS

SHORT STORY (FICTION)

Answers:

1. c) Making school kinder
2. b) To help lonely kids
3. a) Liam was observant and caring
4. d) By the end, even shy kids were smiling and laughing
5. b) Showing kindness helps everyone feel included

INFORMATIONAL PARAGRAPH (NONFICTION)

Answers:
1. b) Arctic
2. b) Thick fur and fat
3. d) Polar bears' home is shrinking because of climate change
4. c) Seals
5. a) To explain how polar bears live and what threatens them

POEM – "SPRING DANCE"

Answers:
1. c) Spring's joy
2. b) Personification
3. a) Happy and playful
4. c) Nature acts like people in the poem
5. b) To help readers imagine spring in a fun way

 ANSWERS

DIALOGUE (PLAY SCRIPT) – "THE LOST LUNCH"

Answers:

1. b) Lost her money
2. b) Returns her money
3. a) Honest and kind
4. d) She thanks Ethan and is happy
5. c) Honesty and helping others are important

PRACTICAL TEXT (RECIPE)

Answers:

1. b) Mix ingredients
2. b) ½ cup
3. d) 1 hour
4. c) 2 cups
5. a) To give directions for making a snack

conclusion

Congratulations! You've just completed the 4th Grade Reading Comprehension Workbook, and that's a huge achievement! 🎉

Throughout this workbook, you explored:

- Exciting fiction stories that sparked your imagination and helped you understand characters, themes, and emotions.
- Real-world nonfiction passages that taught you about science, nature, history, and important people who changed the world.
- Social-emotional stories that built your empathy, confidence, and decision-making skills.
- Vocabulary builders that gave you the tools to understand new words and use them with confidence.
- Comprehension practice that sharpened your thinking through multiple-choice and open-ended questions.

Each chapter was designed to:

✅ Strengthen your reading and thinking skills
✅ Build your vocabulary and language power
✅ Help you make connections between stories and real life
✅ Prepare you for success in school and beyond

Whether you were solving a mystery in The Magic Compass, learning about The Life of a Honeybee, or thinking about tough choices in The Big Decision, you were learning how to become a stronger reader, a better thinker, and a more thoughtful person.

⭐ **Keep Going!**

This is just the beginning. The more you read, the more you'll grow. Keep exploring books, asking questions, and trying new stories. Reading isn't just about answers—it's about discovery, creativity, and understanding the world around you.

Thank you for taking this journey with us.
Happy reading and keep turning the pages!

APPENDIX -A :
COMMON READING COMPREHENSION QUESTION STARTERS

Question Type	Question Starter
Main Idea	What is the main idea of this passage?
Supporting Detail	Which detail supports the main idea?
Sequence of Events	What happened first/next/last?
Character Traits	What kind of person is the character?
Character Motivation	Why did the character do that?
Cause and Effect	What caused this to happen?
Compare and Contrast	How are these things alike or different?
Inference	What can you guess about this character?
Vocabulary in Context	What does this word mean in the sentence?
Author's Purpose	Why did the author write this text?

APPENDIX -B :
SIGNAL WORDS FOR TEXT STRUCTURES

Text Structure	Signal Words
Cause and Effect	because, since, as a result, therefore
Compare and Contrast	like, unlike, similarly, however, but
Chronological Order	first, next, then, after, finally
Problem and Solution	problem, solution, solve, dilemma, answer
Description	for example, such as, including, characteristics
Sequence/Process	steps, procedure, begin, continue, end
Classification	types, categories, group, belongs
Generalization	always, never, all, most, usually
Opinion and Argument	I believe, in my opinion, should, must
Question and Answer	who, what, when, where, why, how

APPENDIX - C : CONTEXT CLUE TYPES AND CLUE WORDS

Clue Type	Clue Words or Hints
Definition	is, means, refers to
Synonym	or, also known as, in other words
Antonym	unlike, but, however, although
Example	such as, for example, like
Inference	clues from the whole sentence or paragraph
Comparison	similar to, just like, likewise
Cause and Effect	because, so, due to
Restatement	stated again in a new way
Punctuation Clues	commas, dashes, parentheses around definitions
Tone Clues	look at the author's mood or attitude

APPENDIX - D : VOCABULARY BUILDER - WORDS FOR COMPREHENSION

Word	Meaning	Use in a Sentence
Predict	To guess what will happen	I predict it will rain later.
Describe	To tell in detail	Please describe the setting.
Identify	To find or point out	Identify the main idea.
Explain	To make something clear	Explain why she was sad.
Support	To give evidence	Support your answer with a detail.
Compare	To tell how things are alike	Compare the two animals.
Contrast	To tell how things are different	Contrast their reactions.
Summarize	To tell the main points briefly	Summarize the chapter in 3 sentences.
Infer	To figure out using clues	Infer how the character is feeling.
Conclude	To decide after thinking	What can you conclude from the story?

YOUNG WRITER SERIES - DR. FANATOMY

Please let us know how we're doing by leaving us a review.

www.ingramcontent.com/pod-product-compliance
Lightning Source LLC
Chambersburg PA
CBHW081403070526
44583CB00020B/2655